EXTREMELY ACCURATE

Birds

A Little Guide

TOMMY SIEGEL

RP MINIS

PHILADELPHIA

RP Minis®
Hachette Book Group
1290 Avenue of the Americas, New York, NY 10104
www.runningpress.com
@Running_Press

First Edition: April 2026

Published by RP Minis, an imprint of Hachette Book Group, Inc. The RP Minis name and logo is a registered trademark of Hachette Book Group, Inc.

Contact specialmarkets@hbgusa.com regarding special discounts for bulk purchases.

Design by Tanvi Baghele

ISBN: 979-8-89414-019-3

Made in Dongguan, China (HKD) 12/25 #01

Contents

FIG. 1

FIG. 2

Introduction

As a cartoonist, I have always had a weakness: realism. While on hiatus from drawing comics a couple of years ago, I became an avid birder and wanted to challenge myself to draw true-to-life birds. While snug in a cabin in the woods in Virginia, I decided to make an attempt at an accurate Hermit Thrush (fig. 1), which I had been admiring earlier in the day.

After posting it on social media, a stranger suggested that I hadn't drawn the legs accurately, so I took a second stab at it (fig. 2).

From that point onward, no one seemed to have any criticism of my work!

As an illustrator, I try my best to be as anatomically precise as possible, which can be quite challenging with only fleeting glimpses of these beautiful species. Because birds' legs and rears are nearly impossible to photograph, I have been forced to make educated scientific

Inexplicable
stick figure legs

Strong,
agile legs

guesses as to what their beautiful legs and posteriors might look like had I been blessed with a better vantage point or the luxury of time. Rather than the place-holder stick-figure-like legs in other volumes, I have opted to illustrate how their legs *must* appear based on their remarkable athletic abilities. Considering I am not a professional ornithologist, I think the results are extremely accurate and I hope you'll agree!

AMERICAN ROBIN

Robins tout gorgeous red breasts and sociable natures that make them one of the only birds that non-birders can immediately identify. Comically, the robin's name is simply the result of someone who didn't know much about birds—what Europeans know as a "robin" is an adorable little flycatcher with a red breast with little else in common with our robin! A colonist must have seen the red breast on our iconic North American thrush and assumed it was the same bird, despite the American Robin being more than twice as large as the European Robin. A beginner birding ID mistake with long-reaching consequences!

Similar species: The Eastern Towhee is smaller with a stouter bill and a white belly.

Size: About the size of, well, a robin!

BARN SWALLOW

Odds are, this illustration is about as good of a look as you'll ever get at a Barn Swallow. Living much of their existence in flight, barn swallows are acrobatic and sensationally agile fliers with distinctive forked tails, blue upper parts, and a chestnut throat. Swooping and lunging in search of insects with their gorgeous legs silhouetted in the sun, they move so fast and unceasingly that they are often mistaken for bats at dusk!

Similar species: Cliff Swallows share the Barn Swallows' underparts and rusty-colored throat but have a distinct white ring around their necks.

Size: About the size of a sparrow.

CALIFORNIA SCRUB-JAY

East Coasters, think of this blue beauty as the Blue Jay of the Pacific. And what a clever jay it is, often observed stealthily stealing acorns from other birds' stashes when they're not looking. And that cleverness is crucial—you can't win a beauty pageant without answering some interview questions, after all! This inquisitive bird is often seen scavenging in open habitats, and its flexible omnivorous diet is well suited to survive the impediments of human development.

Similar species: The Woodhouse's Scrub-Jay is quite similar, but its range pushes farther east into the Southwest's desert habitats and the southeastern Rockies.

Size: Larger than a robin, smaller than a crow.

BLUE-GRAY GNATCATCHER

Often heard but not seen, the tiny Blue-gray Gnatcatcher has a distinctively squeaky call and a nasal song that can often act as your only clue to its whereabouts. It took me years of birding until I saw one out in the open! To make matters even more exciting, this gorgeous blue-gray bird was hopping erratically through the outer foliage, hunting for scrumptious spiders by flicking its long, gorgeous tail. I came to learn this tail twitching was a common gnatcatcher activity to scare up insects for a snack, but in that moment I thought I was simply receiving a private and lurid dance. Foolish me!

Similar species: If in the desert, keep an eye out for the Black-tailed Gnatcatcher.

Size: Slightly smaller than a sparrow.

Female: More grayish above.

NORTHERN CARDINAL

Though a common sight in the eastern half of North America, witnessing a Northern Cardinal's handsome red body still steals my breath away at nearly every sighting, but especially against the backdrop of snow. Large, bold, and gregarious songbirds that defend their territory intensely from other males, they nest in dense tangles of shrubs. The inviting and spunky Northern Cardinal brightens any winter day, and clearly I'm not alone in this opinion; this spunky bird is the official bird of seven U.S. states!

Size: Larger than a sparrow, smaller than a robin.

Female: Distinctly different and brown overall, with only tinges of red.

DARK-EYED JUNCO

This Dark-eyed Junco isn't leaving much to the imagination, and thank goodness! This adorable, plump, and common bird with its distinct pink bill regularly delights eager birders like me in the winter. Often seen on the ground, they bounce around the bases of trees looking for seeds. You'll notice a slightly different look with a distinct head delineation if you see one out West—those were previously considered to be a different species! In fact, their slight regional differences in appearance were formerly thought to be *five* different species in total.

Size: Sparrow size.

CEDAR WAXWING

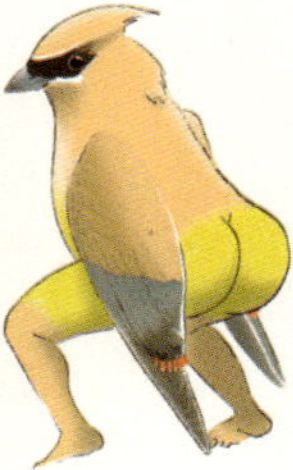

The fabulous Cedar Waxwing renders me dazzled with shock at every sighting, and it's not hard to see why. A silky mixture of brown, gray, and lemon yellow (and even a "waxy" flash of red in the droplets at their wingtips), they may be the most handsome and visually stimulating bird on the entire continent.

Acrobatic, exciting, and flamboyant, they are fruit lovers who gobble berries in large groups, often identified from a distance by their thin, lispy cries. A sociable bird, it's rare to see one by itself, so you'll often see a line of Cedar Waxwings passing a berry back and forth until one of them swallows it. Oh, what a sublime pleasure it would be to trade berries with these inviting and fruity birds in a berry conga line!

Size: Larger than a sparrow, smaller than a robin.

WESTERN TANAGER

Oh no! Is that adorable songbird engulfed in flames? No, it's simply the gorgeous, orange-red radiance of the male Western Tanager's head! Though common in open woods all over the west, you're still quite lucky to catch a lingering glimpse of one, as they spend most of their time hidden in the evergreen canopy. And if you do spy one through your binoculars, try not to stare directly at its fiery radiance; you might get burned!

Similar species: Keep an eye out for the Summer Tanager, which can be quite similar to Western Tanager females and non-breeding males.

Size: Larger than a sparrow, smaller than a robin.

Female: Duller yellow and lacks the brilliant orange-red head.

COOPER'S HAWK

If you see a hawk sitting upright and staring at your bird feeder, odds are it's the fearsome but modest-size Cooper's Hawk. Compared to other hawks like the lesser-seen and visibly smaller Sharp-shinned Hawk, you can distinguish the Cooper's Hawk by its relatively large head and rounded tail. This striking and common hawk feeds mostly on, well . . . other birds, captured in flight! Vicious hunters, they are known to squeeze their prey to death with their muscular feet and are often observed drowning birds to death by holding them underwater.

Similar species: As mentioned, the Sharp-shinned Hawk is notably smaller, rounder-headed, and much less common in suburban areas.

Size: About the size of a crow.

RUBY-THROATED HUMMINGBIRD

A flash of green! No, wait, a flash of red! You gasp aloud as you realize your feeder has been blessed by the flirtatious and electrifying Ruby-throated Hummingbird as it hums and slurps nectar. Eastern North America's sole breeding hummingbird, they glitter like an emerald in the sun, then vanish in a blink. They beat their wings over fifty times a second, but I suspect the pace of my heartbeat is even faster when this glamorous pixie bewitches my feeder! In the fall, they zip and zigzag their way to Mexico and Central America, where they treat our southern friends to the same salacious and zippy show that we have the honor of witnessing from the comfort of our back porches.

Similar species: There are at least seven other common hummingbirds out West, including the Rufous Hummingbird, the Black-chinned Hummingbird, Allen's Hummingbird, the Broad-tailed Hummingbird, and Anna's Hummingbird.

Size: Smaller than a sparrow, larger than a bee!

Female: Lacks the male's ruby throat. Green on the head and back with a white belly.